Dec. 2009.

May the wisdom
of the words within
this book bring
you comfort.

Love Sandy

D0475364

Words *of* Wisdom
from the Dalai Lama

Words *of* Wisdom
from the Dalai Lama

Quotes by His Holiness

Compiled by
MARGARET GEE

GRAMERCY BOOKS
NEW YORK

This 2005 edition is published by Gramercy Books, an imprint of Random House Value Publishing, a division of Random House, Inc., New York, by arrangement with Andrews McMeel Publishing.

Gramercy is a registered trademark and the colophon is a trademark of Random House, Inc.

Random House
New York • Toronto • London • Sydney • Auckland
www.randomhouse.com

Printed and bound in the United States.

Library of Congress Cataloging-in-Publication Data

Bstan-'dzin-rgya-mtsho, Dalai Lama XIV, 1935-
    Words of wisdom from the Dalai Lama : quotes by His Holiness the
Dalai Lama / compiled by Margaret Gee.
        p. cm.
    Originally published as: Words of wisdom, selected quotes from His
Holiness the Dalai Lama. Kansas City: Andrews McMeel Pub., 2001.
    ISBN 0-517-22379-1
    1. Bstan-®'zin-rgya-mtsho, Dalai Lama XIV, 1935—Quotations. I.
Gee, Margaret. II. Title.

BQ7935.B77B77 2005
294.3'923—dc22

                                        2004054077

10 9 8 7 6 5 4 3 2 1

For my parents, Allan and Kath,
who were wise and loving.

I would like to sincerely thank
Namgyel Tsering
for his invaluable assistance
in compiling this book.

FOREWORD

I am honored and pleased to introduce Margaret Gee's revised publication of *Words of Wisdom*.

This book is a compilation of His Holiness the Dalai Lama's powerful message of wisdom. His Holiness is respected and loved not only by the Tibetans but by millions of people around the world.

He has touched the hearts of the people, transcending religious and political barriers. I believe that his message contained in this book will encourage and inspire readers.

Namgyel Tsering
President, Australian Tibetan Society

HIS HOLINESS THE DALAI LAMA

The Dalai Lama, Tenzin Gyatso, is the spiritual and temporal leader of the Tibetan people. He was born on 6 July 1935, in a small village called Taktser in northeastern Tibet. Born to a peasant family, His Holiness was recognized at the age of two, in accordance with Tibetan tradition, as the reincarnation of his predecessor, the thirteenth Dalai Lama.

The Dalai Lamas are the manifestations of the Buddha of Compassion, who chose to take rebirth for the purpose of serving other human beings. *Dalai Lama* means "Ocean of Wisdom." Tibetans normally refer to His Holiness as Yeshe Norbu, "the Wish-fulfilling Gem," or simply Kundun, meaning "the Presence."

In 1933, when the thirteenth Dalai Lama passed away, the task that confronted the Tibetan Government was not simply to appoint a successor but to seek for and discover a child in whom the Buddha of

Compassion would incarnate. It was not necessary that the child should have been born just at the time of the death of his predecessor, or even soon after.

As on former such occasions, there would be indications of the directions in which the search should be made, and signs that the child would be found to possess physical and mental attributes similar to those of his predecessor.

In 1935, the Regent of Tibet went to the sacred lake of Lhamoe Lhatso, about ninety miles southeast of Lhasa, Tibet's capital. The Tibetans have observed that visions of the future can be seen in this lake. The regent saw the vision of three Tibetan letters: *Ah*, *Ka*, and *Ma*, followed by a picture of a monastery with roofs of jade green and gold and a house with turquoise tiles. A detailed description of these visions was written down and kept a strict secret.

In 1937, high lamas and dignitaries, carrying the secrets of the visions, were sent to all parts of Tibet to search for the place that the Regent had seen in the waters. The search party that headed east, toward Taktser, was under the leadership of Lama Kewtsang Rinpoche of Sera Monastery. When they arrived in the province of Amdo, they found a place matching the description of the secret vision. The party went to the house, which was the Gyatso home, with Kewtsang

Rinpoche disguised as a servant and a junior official, Lobsang Tsewang, disguised as the leader. The lama was wearing a rosary that had belonged to the thirteenth Dalai Lama; the little boy, recognizing it, demanded that it should be given to him. Kewtsang Rinpoche asked who the leader was, and the boy replied that he was Sera Aga, which meant, in the local dialect, "a lama of Sera." Kewtsang Rinpoche then asked for the name of the leader, and the boy gave his name correctly. He also knew the name of the real servant. This was followed by a series of tests, which included choosing, from among several articles, those that had belonged to the thirteenth Dalai Lama. By these tests, the members of the search party were further convinced that the reincarnation had been found, and their conviction was enhanced by the vision of three letters: *Ah* stood for Amdo, the name of the province; *Ka* stood for Kumbum, one of the largest monasteries in the neighborhood. The two letters *Ka* and *Ma* also stood for the monastery of Karma Rolpai Dorjee, on the mountain above the village. It was also significant that once the thirteenth Dalai Lama had stayed at the monastery on his way back from China. In 1940, the new Dalai Lama was enthroned.

He began his education at the age of six. At twenty-four, His Holiness took the preliminary examinations at each of the three monastic universities: Drepung, Sera, and Ganden. The final examination was held in the Jokhang, Lhasa, during the annual Monlam Festival of prayer, which occurs during the first month of each year. In the morning he was examined on logic by thirty different scholars. In the afternoon, fifteen scholars took part as his opponents in the debate on the Middle Path, and in the evening thirty-five scholars tested his knowledge of the canon of monastic discipline and the study of metaphysics. His Holiness passed the examination with honors. He completed the Geshe Lharampa degree (doctorate of Buddhist philosophy) when he was twenty-five.

In 1950, when he was only sixteen, he had been called upon to assume full political power because Tibet was threatened by the might of China. In 1954, His Holiness went to Beijing for peace talks with Mao Tse-tung and other Chinese leaders, including Chou En-lai and Deng Xiaoping. In 1956, His Holiness visited India to attend the 2,500th Buddha Jayanti anniversary. While in India, His Holiness had a series of meetings with Prime Minister Nehru and Premier Chou En-lai about deteriorating conditions in Tibet.

In 1959, His Holiness was forced into exile in India after the Chinese military occupation of Tibet. Since that time, His Holiness has been residing near Dharmsala, in northern India—the seat of the Tibetan government in exile.

While in exile, His Holiness has appealed to the United Nations on the question of Tibet, resulting in three resolutions being adopted by the General Assembly, in 1959, 1961, and 1965.

His Holiness has set up educational, cultural, and religious institutions that have contributed significantly toward the preservation of the Tibetan identity and its rich heritage. In 1963, His Holiness promulgated a draft constitution for Tibet that ensures a democratic form of government. Unlike his predecessors, His Holiness has traveled to North and South America, Czechoslovakia, Europe, the United Kingdom, Japan, Thailand, and Australia and has met with religious leaders from these countries.

During his travels abroad, His Holiness has spoken out strongly for better understanding and respect among the different faiths of the world. Toward this end, His Holiness has made numerous appearances in interfaith services, imparting the message of universal responsibility, love, compassion, and kindness. "The need for simple human-to-human relationship is becoming increasingly urgent. . . . Today the world is smaller and more interdependent. One nation's problems can no longer be solved by itself completely.

Thus, without a sense of universal responsibility, our very survival becomes threatened. Basically, universal responsibility is feeling for other people's suffering just as we feel our own. It is the realization that even our enemy is entirely motivated by the quest for happiness. We must recognize that all beings want the same thing that we want. This is the way to achieve a true understanding, unfettered by artificial consideration" (*Tibetan History and Culture*, Australian Tibetan Society).

In 1989 His Holiness was awarded the Nobel Peace Prize for his consistent opposition to the use of violence, even in the face of aggression to his people. Numerous other awards have been bestowed upon him. His Holiness the Dalai Lama is loved and respected worldwide as a man of peace.

Since His Holiness was awarded the Nobel Peace Prize he has achieved several important diplomatic breakthroughs, including historic meetings with President George Bush—the first U.S. president to meet with the Dalai Lama (April 1991)—and British Prime Minister John Major (December 1991).

He has been welcomed by many world leaders, including the pope, Nelson Mandela, and President Clinton. From 1986 on the Dalai Lama has held a series of "Mind and Life" discussions with leading

Western researchers to explore the links between modern science and the Tibetan Buddhist understanding of phenomena such as the mind, dreams, disease, conception, and death.

A scholar, a man of peace, and a spokesman for better understanding among people and religions, the Dalai Lama travels widely, giving Buddhist teachings and initiations and imparting the message of love, compassion, kindness, and universal responsibility.

Among his awards are:

Ramon Magsaysay Award to Community Leadership
  (Philippines), 1959
The Lincoln Award, Research Institute of America
  (USA), 1960
Peace Medal, Asian Buddhist Council for Peace
  (Ulan Bator, Mongolia), 1979
The Albert Schweitzer Humanitarian Award, The
  Human Behavioral Foundation (New York, USA),
  1987
The Dr. Leopold Lucas Prize, University of Tübingen
  (West Germany), 1988
Nobel Peace Prize (Oslo, Norway), 1989
Prix de Mémoire Award (Paris, France), 1989
Humanitarian Award, World Management Council
  (New York, USA), 1989

Raoul Wallenberg Congressional Human Rights
Award (USA), 1989

Earth Prize, United Earth and U.N. Environmental
Program (New York, USA), 1991

Peace and Unity Awards, National Peace Confer-
ence (New Delhi, India), 1991

Honorary Doctorate of Law, Melbourne University
(Australia), 1992

Honorary Fellow, Hebrew University (Israel), 1994

Doctor of Human Letters, Berea College (USA), 1994

Doctor of Human Arts and Letters, Columbia University (USA), 1994

World Security Annual Peace Award, New York
Lawyers' Alliance (USA), 1994

Roosevelt Four Freedoms Award, Franklin and
Eleanor Roosevelt Institute (Middelburg, Hol-
land), 1994

Doctor of Buddhist Philosophy, Honoris Causa
Rissho University (Japan), 1995

Honorary Doctorate of Philosophy, Sun Yat-sen
University (Taiwan), 1997

Some of his many books include: *Freedom in Exile: The
Autobiography of the Dalai Lama; My Land and My People;
Ethics for the New Millennium;* and *The Art of Happiness,* along
with distinguished writings on Buddhist philosophy.

Selected Quotes

Everybody loves to talk about calmness and peace, whether in a family, national, or international context, but without inner peace how can we make real peace? World peace through hatred and force is impossible.

Because we all share an identical need for love, it is possible to feel that anybody we meet, in whatever circumstances, is a brother or sister.

In my childhood, I had a religious assistant who always told me, if you can really laugh with full abandonment, it's very good for your health.

The main cause of suffering is egoistic desire for one's own comfort and happiness.

We must all live harmoniously with our neighbors.

My religion is very simple.
My religion is kindness.

On a daily basis, you must take more care of
your mind than just money, money, money!

In this century we have made remarkable material progress, but basically we are the same as
we were thousands of years ago. Our spiritual
needs are still very great.

In the interests of everyone the artist has a responsibility to use his medium well. In the Tibetan culture, most of the paintings are of deities or Buddhas, and they try to send a message of the value of the spiritual.

Through meditative techniques, one can free the mind of delusions and attain what we call enlightenment.

We have to adopt a wider perspective, and always find common things between the people of north, east, south, and west. Conflict comes from the basis of differences.

If through practice of insight you develop a sense of ease, then time has no relevance. If you're miserable, time does matter. It's so unbearable, so enormous you want to get out of it as soon as possible.

When a problem first arises, try to remain humble and maintain a sincere attitude, and be concerned that the outcome is fair.

The very purpose of meditation is to discipline the mind and reduce afflictive emotions.

Through money or power you cannot solve all problems. The problem in the human heart must first be solved.

Your enemy is your best friend.

The seed for nirvana exists in all of us. The time has come to think more wisely, hasn't it?

If the mind is dominated by hatred, the best part of the brain, which is used to judge right and wrong, does not function properly.

Feelings of anger, bitterness, and hate are negative. If I kept them inside me they would spoil my body and my health. They are of no use.

For a better, happier, more stable and civilized future, each of us must develop a sincere, warm-hearted feeling of brotherhood and sisterhood.

Freedom is the real source of human happiness and creativity. Irrespective of whether you are a believer or nonbeliever, whether Buddhist, Christian, or Jew, the important thing is to be a good human being.

We have to have some form of politics. Politics is a form of resolving conflicts. Politics which comes from sincere motivation is constructive.

The basic sources of happiness are a good heart, compassion, and love. If we have these mental attitudes, even if we are surrounded by hostility, we feel little disturbance. On the other hand, if we lack compassion and our mental state is filled with anger or hatred we will not have peace.

Ignorance is the source of hatred, and the way to get rid of ignorance is realization.

The ultimate way to solve human problems is with nonviolence.

All religions are essentially the same in their goal of developing a good human heart so that we may become better human beings.

To me there is no difference whether president, beggar, or king.

My mother was very kind, calm, but of course she was illiterate. Later, she learned to read so she could study the scriptures. When we came to Lhasa, I lived separately, but that does not mean I was completely cut off. Whenever she came to see me, she brought me the bread she baked.

The more we care for the happiness of others, the greater our own sense of well-being becomes.

For a person who cherishes compassion and love, the practice of tolerance is essential, and for that, an enemy is indispensable. So we should be grateful to our enemies, for it is they who can best help us develop a tranquil mind.

Indulgence in resentment and vengeance will only further increase miseries to oneself and others in this life and in lives to come.

Humans are not machines—we are something more. We have feeling and experience. Material comforts are not sufficient to satisfy us. We need something deeper—human affection.

No material object, however beautiful or valuable, can make us feel loved, because our deeper identity and true character lie in the subjective nature of the mind.

I am often moved by the example of small insects, such as bees. The laws of nature dictate that bees work together in order to survive. As a result they possess an instinctive sense of social responsibility. They have no constitution, laws, police, religion, or moral training, but because of their nature they labor faithfully together. Occasionally they may fight, but in general the whole colony survives on the basis of cooperation. Human beings, on the other hand, have constitutions, vast legal systems, and police forces. We have religion, remarkable intelligence, and a heart with a great capacity to love. But despite our many extraordinary qualities, in actual practice we lag behind these small insects. In some ways I feel we are poorer than the bees.

Without proper mental peace it is difficult to achieve proper world peace; therefore there is a connection. Many of the problems that we have today are because of our hatred. As human beings we have good qualities as well as bad ones. Now anger, attachment, jealousy, and hatred are the bad side. They are the real enemy. From a certain point of view, our real enemy, the true troublemaker, is inside. I try to see each tragedy in the context of other, bigger tragedies in history. That gives me a larger focus and makes it easier to bear. So that is my secret, my trick. I believe I am a happy person.

The basic Buddhist stand on the question of equality between the genders is age-old. At the highest tantric levels, at the highest esoteric level, you must respect women, every woman.

We need a little more compassion, and if we cannot have it then no politician or even a magician can save the planet.

Without feelings we cannot make a demarcation between justice or injustice, truth or untruth, good or bad.

I believe that constant effort, tireless effort, pursuing clear goals with sincere effort is the only way.

For me it is nothing. New millennium or new century or new year. For me it is another day, another night. The sun, the moon, the stars remain the same.

Although I do not personally have any experience, from talking to people who have taken drugs I have the impression that by taking drugs you lose your discriminative power. This would not be helpful for higher meditation. The mental development should be carried out by internal means, not through external means.

From a believer's point of view I do have some special relationship with some higher beings. But in my own mind I am still an ordinary Buddhist monk.

At times there have been impossible responsibilities and a lot of difficulties. Then again, personally I'm quite jovial with not much worry. I do my best, which is moderation, and failure doesn't matter.

At daybreak if the weather is fine, I go into the garden. This time of day is very special to me. The sky is clear, I see the stars, and I have this special feeling—of my insignificance in the cosmos, the realization of what we Buddhists call impermanence.

In some respects I have been the most unlucky Dalai Lama because I have spent more time living as a refugee outside of my country than I have spent in Tibet. On the other hand, it has been very rewarding for me to live in a democracy and to learn about the world in a way that we Tibetans had never known before.

I just want to live as a simple Buddhist monk, but during that last thirty years I have made many friends around the world and I want to have close contact with these people. I want to contribute to harmony and peace of mind, for less conflict. Wherever the possibility is, I'm ready. This is my life's goal.

In order to achieve genuine, lasting world peace based on compassion, we need a sense of universal responsibility. First, we have to try inner disarmament—reducing our own anger and hatred while increasing mutual trust and human affection.

Even though a bird can fly, it must land on earth.

Our problems, though grave and complex, are within our own power to control and rectify. The solution can only be based upon an approach that transcends selfish and regional demands.

Good human qualities—honesty, sincerity, a good heart—cannot be bought with money, nor can they be produced by machines, but only by the mind itself. We can call this the inner light, or God's blessing, or human quality. This is the essence of mankind.

Around the world millions of people remain silent, but the majority want peace, not bloodshed. Don't worry, I plan to live one hundred years.

If you have a sincere and open heart, you naturally feel self-worth and confidence, and there is no need to be fearful of others. If you have this basic quality of kindness or good heart, then all other things, such as education and ability, will go in the right direction.

There's no shop that sells kindness, you must build it within. You can transplant hearts, but you cannot transplant a warm heart.

If we lose our human values by having everything mechanized, then machines will dictate our lives.

When you encounter some problems, if you point your finger at yourself and not at others, this gives you control over yourself and calmness in a situation, where otherwise self-control becomes problematic.

Infinite altruism is the basis of peace and happiness. If you want altruism, you must control hate and you must practice patience. The main teachers of patience are our enemies.

Because violence can only breed more violence and suffering, our struggle must be nonviolent and free of hatred.

If anything I've said seems useful to you, I'm glad. If not, don't worry. Just forget about it.

If you help and serve others, you will ultimately gain.

When we die nothing can be taken with us
but the seeds of our life's work and our spiritual
knowledge.

Compassion and tolerance are not a sign of
weakness, but a sign of strength.

All human beings come from a mother's womb. We are all the same part of one human family. We should have a clear realization of the oneness of all humanity.

History shows that most of the positive or beneficial developments in human society have occurred as the result of care and compassion. Consider, for example, the abolition of the slave trade. Ideals are the engine of progress.

The rationale for loving others is the recognition of the simple fact that every living being has the same right to and the same desire for happiness, and not suffering, and the consideration that you as one individual are one life unit as compared with the multitude of others in their ceaseless quest for happiness.

The basic sources of happiness are a good heart, compassion, and love. If we have these mental attitudes, even if we are surrounded by hostility, we feel little disturbance. On the other hand, if we lack compassion and our mental state is filled with anger or hatred, we will not have peace.

The unique Tibetan culture produces human beings with more smiles on their faces. The Tibetan character is a little bit different. The tourists say it is a strange experience.

A learned person will become noble only when he or she has put into real practice what has been learned, instead of just mere words.

Some of you feel that you lose your independence if you don't let your mind just wander when it wants to, if you try to control it. But that is not the case. If your mind is proceeding in the correct way, one already has the correct opinion. But if your mind is proceeding in an incorrect way, then it's necessary, definitely, to exercise control.

If we adopt a self-centered approach to life, by which we attempt to use others for our own self interest, we might be able to gain temporary benefits, but in the long run we will not succeed in achieving even our personal happiness, and hope for the next life is out of the question.

A mind that is characterized by unrest will not be tranquil even in the presence of great calm.

I want to say without hesitation that the purpose of our life is happiness.

The true test of honoring Buddhas or God is the love one extends to fellow humans.

Anger and agitation make us more susceptible to illness.

The concept of violence is out of date. The destruction of your neighborhood is actually the destruction of yourself.

We need to give more attention to our inner values.

My religion is kindness. A good mind, a good heart, warm feelings, these are the most important things.

Ha, ha, ha—I am just a simple Buddhist monk.

True enlightenment is nothing but the nature of one's own self being fully realized.

If you are showing love to your fellow human beings, you are showing love to your God.

Anger is the ultimate troublemaker. I feel you can express a strong disapproval or dislike of an object without losing your temper.

Wherever you are, your religious teaching must be there with you.

Firstly, as a Buddhist monk, I hold that violence is not good. Secondly, I am a firm believer in the Gandhian ethic of passive resistance. And thirdly, in reality, violence is not our strength.

If one assumes a humble attitude, one's own good qualities will increase. Whereas if one is proud, one will become jealous of others, one will look down on others, and due to that there will be unhappiness in society.

I think when tragic things happen it is on the surface. It's like the ocean. On the surface a wave comes and sometimes the wave is very serious and strong. But it comes and goes, comes and goes, and underneath, the ocean always remains calm. Tibetans have a saying: "If bad news comes you listen here" (points to the right ear) "and let it out here" (points to the left ear).

In my daily life, I can say that 80 to 90 percent of my energy is expended on religious matters, the remaining 10 to 20 percent on Tibetan problems. So naturally I feel myself primarily to be a religious person. Besides, I have studied religion, I have some experience of religion, so I have some confidence in that respect.

There are two types of competitive behavior. One is a sense of competition because you want to be at the top. You create obstacles and harm someone. That competition is negative. But there is a positive kind of competition which benefits the individual, the competitors, and the economy. Let your competitors also grow, without any sense of harming them.

Sometimes religion becomes yet another source for more division and even open conflict. Because of that situation, I feel the different religious traditions have a great responsibility to provide peace of mind and a sense of brotherhood and sisterhood among humanity.

At the end of the last century, science and spirituality seemed incompatible. Now, they have moved closer together.

It is my fundamental belief that all human beings share the same basic aspirations: that we all want happiness and that we all share suffering. Asians, just like Americans, Europeans, and the rest of the world, share a desire to live life to its fullest, to better ourselves and the lives of our loved ones.

In reality I believe that economic advancement and respect for individual rights are closely linked. Society cannot fully maximize its economic advantage without granting its people civil and political rights.

If you shift your focus from oneself to others, and think more about others' well-being and welfare, it has an immediate liberating effect.

In twenty years' time I'll be eighty-three, just an old man with a stick moving like a sloth bear. While I'm alive, I am fully committed to autonomy, and I am the person who can persuade the Tibetan people to accept it.

From the very core of our being we desire contentment. For harmony each individual's identity must be fully respected.

The two most important things to remember in business are: to be aware of the consequential impact on ecology, and a caring relationship between employer and employee.

Inner darkness, which we call ignorance, is the root of suffering. The more inner light that comes, the more darkness will diminish. This is the only way to achieve salvation or nirvana.

Nonviolence is the only way. Even if you achieve your goal by violent means there are always side effects, and these can be worse than the problem. Violence is against human nature.

If the mind is tranquil and occupied with positive thoughts, the body will not easily fall prey to disease.

It is our enemies who provide us with the challenge we need to develop the qualities of tolerance, patience, and compassion.

Remember, you are a Westerner. If you want to practice an Eastern philosophy such as Tibetan Buddhism you should take the essence and try to adapt it to your cultural background and conditions.

Cultivating a close, warmhearted feeling for others automatically puts the mind at ease. From the least to the most important event, the affection and respect of others are vital for our happiness.

It is important to use money properly to help others; otherwise you will still want more and feel poor.

The essence of Buddhism is if you can, help others. If not, then at least refrain from hurting others.

Mother planet is showing us the red warning light. Be careful, she is saying. To take care of the planet is to take care of our own house.

What is the meaning of life?
To be happy and useful.

Smile if you want a smile from another face.

Religions must serve humanity, not the other way around.

If you have too much expectation, you may come away disappointed.

Love, compassion, and forgiveness—these are the things I preach.